The Cherokee Syllabary

AN ILLUSTRATED KEY TO THE CHEROKEE LANGUAGE

ᏣᏬᏯ ᎵᎠᏬᎶᎵ ᏗᏃᏴᎩ

Tsalagi Digoweli Tsunoyvgi

WRITTEN BY

Brad Wagnon

ILLUSTRATED BY

Beth Anderson

7th GENERATION
Summertown, Tennessee

The Cherokee alphabet is not an alphabet at all but a **syllabary**. That means that each Cherokee character represents a complete syllable, not just a consonant or a vowel. The Cherokee word for "water," pronounced *ama*, is written with three English letters, **a, m,** and **a**. Using the Cherokee syllabary, the same word is written with only two characters: **D**, pronounced *a*, and **Ꮓ** pronounced *ma*.

Accompanying each of the illustrations is a facing page that shows a Cherokee word that contains the illustrated Cherokee syllabary character. The sound of each syllable in the Cherokee word is shown below the corresponding Cherokee character. The English translation of the Cherokee word is shown on the following line.

A row of characters from the Cherokee syllabary chart is shown at the bottom of each page, with each character's corresponding sound below it.

The entire Cherokee syllabary is shown on the next page as a chart. The chart contains a column for each vowel sound; the rows show how those vowel sounds combine with each of the consonant sounds to make a Cherokee syllable.

Basic Pronunciation Key

- **a:** as *a* in "father"
- **e:** as *a* in "cake"
- **i:** as *e* in "Pete"
- **o:** as *o* in "hello"
- **u:** as *u* in "tuba"
- **v:** as *u* in "rung" but with a more nasal sound

All the Cherokee consonant sounds are the same as their English versions with a few exceptions:

- **g:** sounds like the *g* in "gaff" or the *k* in "kite"
- **qu:** sounds like the *qu* in "question" or the *gw* in "Gwen"
- **tl:** non-English sound made by combining *t* or *h* with the *l* sound
- **Ts:** sounds like *j* in "John," or *ch* in "chair"

Note: Dialects will differ, even between communities that are fairly close geographically.

D	**R**	**T**	**Ꮼ**	**Ꮻ**	**i**
a	e	i	o	u	v
Ꮝ **Ꮨ**	**Ᏻ**	**Ꭹ**	**A**	**J**	**E**
ga ka	ge	gi	go	gu	gv
Ꮵ	**Ꮅ**	**Ꭾ**	**Ꮁ**	**Γ**	**Ꮐ**
ha	he	hi	ho	hu	hv
W	**Ꮄ**	**Ꮑ**	**G**	**M**	**Ꮣ**
la	le	li	lo	lu	lv
Ꮤ	**Ꮆ**	**H**	**Ꮒ**	**Ꭻ**	
ma	me	mi	mo	mu	
Ꮎ **Ꮏ** **G**	**Ꮅ**	**ħ**	**Z**	**Ꮕ**	**Ꮝ**
na hna nah	ne	ni	no	nu	nv
Ꮖ	**Ꮗ**	**Ꮘ**	**Ꮙ**	**Ꮚ**	**Ꮛ**
qua	que	qui	quo	quu	quv
Ꮜ **Ꮝ**	**4**	**Ꮢ**	**Ꮥ**	**Ꮧ**	**R**
sa s	se	si	so	su	sv
Ꮧ **W**	**Ꮷ** **Ꮨ**	**Ꮪ** **Ꮫ**	**V**	**S**	**Ꮬ**
da ta	de te	di ti	do/to	du/tu	dv/tv
Ꮭ **Ꮧ**	**L**	**C**	**Ꮲ**	**Ꮳ**	**P**
tla dla	tle	tli	tlo	tlu	tlv
G	**Ꮴ**	**Ꮶ**	**K**	**ᴆ**	**Ꮯ**
tsa	tse	tsi	tso	tsu	tsv
G	**Ꮾ**	**Ꮹ**	**Ꮿ**	**9**	**6**
wa	we	wi	wo	wu	wv
Ꮐ	**ß**	**Ꭹ**	**ꭶ**	**Gʷ**	**B**
ya	ye	yi	yo	yu	yv

a   ma

water

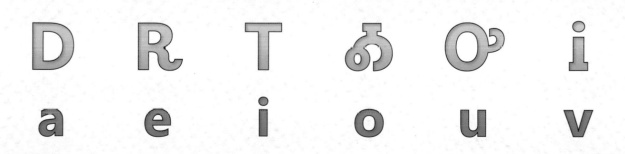

SAGT

ga   lv   lo   i

sky

S F Y A J E

ga   ge   gi   go   gu   gv

ka wi

coffee

ka

ᎤᏆᎾᎢᏗ

ha wi n' di tlv

underground

ᏆᏛ Ᏼ Ꭿ Ᏺ Ᏻ Ᏺ

ha   he   hi   ho   hu   hv

se   lu

corn

Ꮃ Ꮄ Ꮅ Ꮺ Ꮇ Ꮏ

la le li lo lu lv

ka ma ma

butterfly

ma me mi mo mu

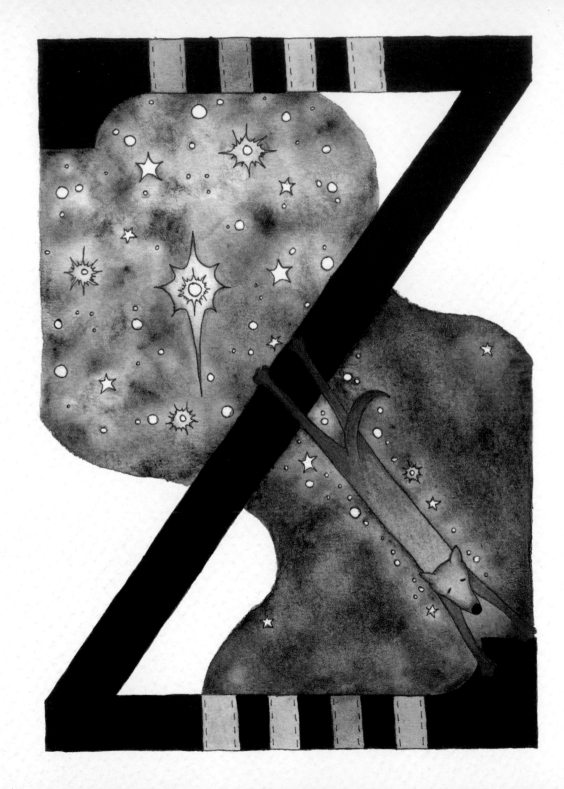

no q' si

star

Θ	Ꮧ	Ꮐ	Ꮑ	Ꮒ	Ꮓ	Ꮔ	Ꮕ
na	hna	nah	ne	ni	no	nu	nv

ЛШҺЛ

di quu yo di

pepper

I ᴕ ᴕ ᴤ ᴕ ᴣ

qua que qui quo quu quv

ᏒᎩ ᎢᎾᎨ ᎡᎯ

sv gi   i na ge   e hi

wild onion

Ꮜ 4 Ꮝ Ꮠ Ꮪ Ꮢ

sa   se   si   so   su   sv

s   ga   du   gi

community

s

ᏚᏗᏅᏔ

da g' si

turtle

Ꮧ Ꮦ Ꮣ Ꮩ Ꮬ ᏅᎧ

da de di do du dv

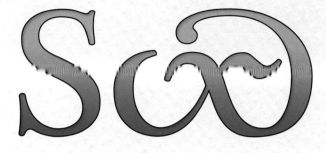

tu ya

beans

Ꮃ Ꮟ Ꭻ Ꮴ Ꮪ Ꮧ

ta te ti to tu tv

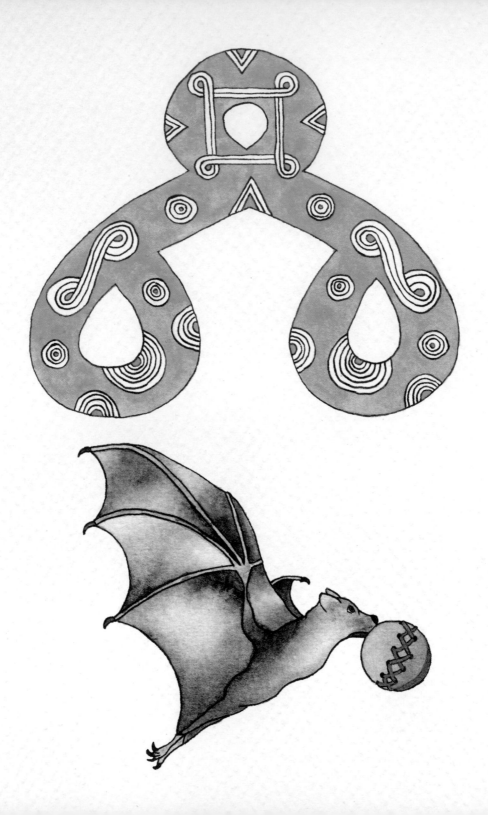

dla me ha

bat

dla

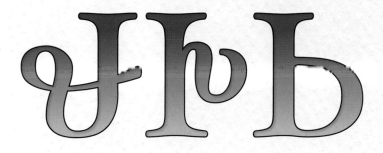

tlo   ge   si

field

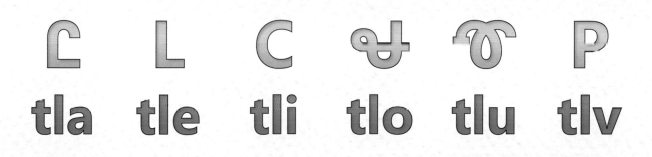

tla   tle   tli   tlo   tlu   tlv

KW

tso   la

tobacco

Ꮳ	Ꮴ	Ꮵ	Ꮶ	Ꮷ	Ꮸ
tsa	tse	tsi	tso	tsu	tsv

wa   ya

wolf

Ꮖ	Ꮗ	Ꮘ	Ꮙ	Ꮚ	Ꮛ
wa	we	wi	wo	wu	wv

ᏲᏂ

yo na

bear

Ꮹ Ꮺ Ꮻ Ꮼ Ꮽ Ᏼ

ya ye yi yo yu yv

About the Artist

Beth Anderson is a Cherokee Nation citizen and a contemporary visual artist. Her work is influenced by her culture, her love of materials and handmade objects, and her relationship with nature. Beth holds a BFA in sculpture from Stephen F. Austin State University in Nacogdoches, Texas, and is certified by the Cherokee Nation Tribal Employment Rights Office (TERO). She is a member of the US Department of Interior's Indian Arts and Crafts Board and is a board member and the Social Media Chair of the Southeastern Indian Artists Association. Beth currently lives in Upstate New York. You can contact her at waterbirdarts@yahoo.com.

About the Author

Brad Wagnon, author, and storyteller is a citizen of the Cherokee Nation. He taught Cherokee history, culture, and language at Tahlequah High School for ten years. Brad has a degree from Northeastern State University in Criminal Justice and Native American Studies. Brad works for Cherokee Nation Emergency Management as the Community Preparedness Coordinator. He has a passion for sharing Cherokee History and Culture with future generations and has authored three Cherokee children's books based on traditional Cherokee stories: *How the World Was Made: A Cherokee Story, The Land of the Great Turtles,* and *The First Fire: A Cherokee Story.* Brad lives in Gideon, OK with his wife Tanya and right next door to his mom on the same property where he grew up. You can contact Brad at bradwagnoncco@gmail.com.

Library of Congress Cataloging-in-Publication Data available upon request.

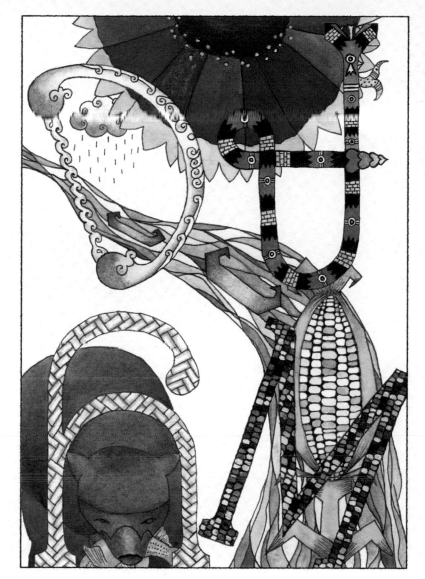

About the Book

We created this book to give Cherokee children the opportunity to see their language in a similar way that English-speaking children have been able to see theirs for centuries. The concept for the illustrations was influenced by medieval illuminated manuscripts. Our intent was to allow Cherokee people of all ages to appreciate and celebrate their wonderful language. We hope you and your children enjoy this beautiful new learning tool.

BRAD AND BETH

7th Generation
Book Publishing Company
PO Box 99, Summertown, TN 38483
888-260-8458
bookpubco.com
nativevoicesbooks.com

29 28 27 26 25 24   1 2 3 4 5 6 7 8 9

Sequoyah was raised by his Cherokee mother, Wuh-teh of the Paint clan, in what is now Tennessee. He never learned to speak, read, or write English, but he was an accomplished silversmith, painter, and warrior. He believed the secret of the white people's superior power was their written language. From 1809 to 1821, Sequoyah created the Cherokee syllabary, which brought literacy to his tribe. Word about the invention of the syllabary quickly spread, and within months, thousands of Cherokees became literate. The simplicity of his system enabled pupils to rapidly learn it, and soon Cherokees throughout the nation were teaching it in their schools and publishing books and newspapers in their own Cherokee language.